CHESAPEAKE PERSPECTIVES

HERITAGE MATTERS

Heritage, Culture, History, and Chesapeake Bay

ERVE CHAMBERS
Department of Anthropology
University of Maryland, College Park

Sea Grant

A Maryland Sea Grant Publication

Publication Number
UM-SG-CP-2006-02

The publication of *Chesapeake Perspectives* is made possible in part by a grant to Maryland Sea Grant from the National Oceanic and Atmospheric Administration, Department of Commerce, through the National Sea Grant College Program. Grant number   NA 05OAR4171042.

Cover and page ix photographs by Harold Anderson.
Book and cover design by Sandy Rodgers.

For more information on this or other publications, or about our program, contact:

Maryland Sea Grant College
University of Maryland
4321 Hartwick Road, Suite 300
College Park, Maryland 20740
www.mdsg.umd.edu

Library of Congress Cataloging-in-Publication Data

Chambers, Erve.
    Heritage matters : heritage, culture, history, and Chesapeake Bay / Erve Chambers.
        p. cm. — (Chesapeake perspectives)
    Includes bibliographical references.
    ISBN-13: 978-0-943676-66-1 (alk. paper)
    ISBN-10: 0-943676-66-5 (alk. paper)
    1. Human ecology—Chesapeake Bay Region (Md. and Va.) 2. Nature—Effect of human beings on—Chesapeake Bay Region (Md. and Va.) 3. Chesapeake Bay Region (Md. and Va.)—Social life and customs. I. Title.
    GF41.C43 2006
    975.2—dc22   2006029573

Contents

*There is nothing that promotes thinking about the past
as well as a poor fishing day, when the water is calm,
the sun keeps your brain from planning your future, and
you are left with nothing but memories.*

— William H. Turner
East of the Chesapeake

Preface

Those who have spent time on or around the Chesapeake Bay have a sense of its wildness, its history, its heritage. Our fondness for the Bay and its quaint communities has found expression in a growing assortment of books, paintings, photographs, postcards, and other memorabilia. Anthropologist Erve Chambers argues that while the attraction of the Bay and our affection for it are genuine, we run the risk of locking the real inhabitants of Bay country into a rigid mold trapped by the very past we celebrate.

As an anthropologist Chambers is interested in the vibrant reality of communities as they experience (and cope with) life. He is also fascinated by the tension between this dynamic reality and the celebrated past, what we often refer to as "heritage." What is heritage really? And who decides what we, as a country or a culture, will celebrate as our treasured past? These are the questions Chambers takes on in this *Chesapeake Perspectives* monograph. He approaches the issue with rigor and a toughness of mind that may at times startle us, as he forces us to think more deeply about what heritage means, and about our own views of the Bay, its past, and its people.

— Jonathan G. Kramer and
Jack Greer, editors

Foreword

Like virtually every other interest-rich place on earth, the Chesapeake Bay is becoming reconfigured in the shapes and musings of a vigorously imagined and sometimes deeply contested heritage. What is involved is much greater than a simple increase in our appreciation of the region's varied histories, traditions, and natural places. Before us are the elements of a major transformation in our thinking about what the Bay is and what it represents — a transformation as profound and far-reaching as the early 17th century entrance of the Chesapeake Bay populace into a burgeoning world market economy.

The effects of the re-invention of the Chesapeake Bay region into the terms represented by our modern concepts of heritage can be as difficult to discern as it would have been to try to predict the outcomes of earlier transformations. And it is equally difficult to believe from our present vantage point that such effects could be anywhere near as profound, although they certainly are. Heritage is no longer embodied simply in faint memories and nostalgia, or embedded principally in the close and "natural" ties of kinship and community. It has become a major conceptual tool in the imagining of our futures, serving in multiple ways to redefine our places and reform our environments, and in some respects also threatening to disrupt those intimate associations of people and their places that have lent familiarity and a measure of continuity to our lives.

This essay goes beyond a consideration of the heritage of the Chesapeake Bay region to the uses of heritage and heritage concepts in a broader context. Still, I have undertaken this writing while considering aspects of the Chesapeake Bay's heritage, particularly as that heritage is expressed through various practices of tourism. While my observations may not always be explicitly about the Chesapeake Bay, they certainly are inspired by my experience of the Bay.

— Erve Chambers

HERITAGE MATTERS

Heritage, Culture, History, and Chesapeake Bay

The Ambiguity of Heritage

Whether on the Chesapeake Bay or anywhere else, the notion of heritage seems ever-present these days. It is a concept that on its surface appears to be perfectly obvious in its meaning, but that begins to unravel before our eyes when we try to associate it with any degree of particularity. Like art *(I don't know what it is, but I know what I like)* or pornography *(I can't define it, but I know it when I see it)*, heritage has become one of those ideas that easily commands our respect and attention, but that in the end does not seem to work in any general sense because its most profound meanings are almost invariably personal and thoroughly partisan. There is no objective sense of heritage to be had. There is no clear and easy way to pronounce with any measure of convincing completeness all of those practices, relationships, and obligations that travel the distances between our pasts and presents.

We might be content and well advised to leave it at that, if it were not for the fact that no one else does. And here the analogies with art and pornography still seem to work. "Heritage" has become a vital addition to the modern places we all inhabit. It is a major industry of the mind as well as of the pocketbook, and has become an increasingly important part of the imagery through which our institutions try to anchor us against the fast pace and uncertainty of our time, to shield us from the seemingly rootless and transient after-effects of modernity and globalization.

Interestingly enough, this emergent transience could well be placing us closer to how humans lived some thousands of years ago, before the agricultural revolution, after which we all became more settled in our ways. Before agriculture, people were principally hunters and gatherers, with a past that they likely carried along as easily as they packed and conveyed their minimal belongings. Their sense of heritage had to be much more direct and intimate, a kind of natural and immediate *inheritance* in which particular skills, human and terrestrial relationships, and important matters of the spirit were more valuable bequests than were gifts of property and accumulated wealth.

The more recent and self-conscious ideas of heritage that we now entertain can be thought of as a way to try to retain the millennia of settled existence that followed these more shifting times. Our instinct is to attempt to slow things down and keep ourselves still settled and hopefully also civilized. But since actually slowing things down is probably not a practical option, what we are left with is the invention of particular "heritages" and assumptions of descent or lineage that permit us to situate ourselves within a past without having to impede the future. Heritage has largely become an instrument that defines the disturbances, irregularities, and uncertainties of the present much more than it truly represents the past. But then, over the last couple of centuries or so, the most significant thing about heritage has not been what it might come to represent, but rather who gets to represent it and to what intent.

In this essay I want to focus on two current possibilities for thinking about heritage. To simplify this distinction I will refer to them as *public* and *private* forms of heritage.

Public Heritage. The first way to approach heritage is as an expression of the past that attempts to preserve important though often fading social practices and, increasingly, also natural processes (as is conveyed in the idea of a "natural heritage"). The basis of this approach to heritage is both preservation and celebration of diversity — the diversity of cultural themes and the diversity of natural things and places.

In contrast to some earlier ideas about heritage, which were more closely linked to ideologies associated with the rise of national identity, and were strengthened by a fairly uncritical faith in the merits of progress, this more recent sense of heritage aims to preserve or at least recognize the passing of distinct cultural practices, many of which are representative of minority or marginalized human populations, as well as to memorialize the possibility of once pristine or at least somewhat "unspoiled" and restorative natural environments. There are obvious benefits to be gained from the more recent perspective, which aims to democratize and broaden our sense of the past. But there are also dangers, the greatest of which is that we might declare the past in such a public way as to make its personally meaningful recovery impossible. This currently prevailing, public treatment of heritage can unintentionally become a way to separate the objects and performances of heritage from their actual heirs, serving to transfer them to the marketplace as commodities — properties and experiences to be appreciated and accumulated by strangers who may well benefit from the association, but who generally have no stake in the outcome and feel little or no responsibility for the kind of careful upkeep that heritage truly requires.

Private Heritage. A second approach encourages us to focus on the ways in which the past is dynamically linked to the present, with heritage values identified and interpreted by community members rather than by outsiders. In this sense, our participation in heritage does not need to be expressed solely in terms of attempts to recover or memorialize a past that has been lost. This brand of heritage is at least equally well understood as a reflection upon the resilience of human and natural places — and their innate inseparability. Important here is the idea that heritage remains linked to existing social processes and environmental conditions. This heritage might still serve as a celebration of something in the past, but its vitality resides in its demonstrable relationship to the present and even to the future. Heritage is in this sense a kind of direct and inalienable inheritance of human and environmental properties and relationships, which might well be appreciated by outsiders but cannot be claimed or possessed by them.[1]

The first and more common sense of heritage described above derives from a close association with history. The value of historical understanding is often promoted as a means of learning from the past, and hopefully of somehow avoiding the mistakes of the past. The past is meaningful in large part because it is perceived (and presented) to be different from the present. Historical thinking tends to encourage us to think in terms of contrasts and differences.

The second sense of heritage described above is invested in the idea of culture. It encourages us to disassociate heritage from the stricter confines of history at least to the extent that we might begin to view heritage not as lessons taught us by duly recognized keepers of the past but as heritable obligations, responsibilities, and privileges that are experienced and repeated in the culture of everyday life, generally in such a way as to subsume the past in the present so thoroughly as to leave unrecognized any significant differences between the two. In this latter sense, "heritage understanding" is bound to suggest something quite different from "historical understanding."

This distinction is important because the idea of heritage has crept into modern consciousness to such an extent that it has begun to play a major role in how we conceive the world in which we live, reshaping our relationships to each other and to our environments. What I suggest here is that we have become accustomed to associating heritage almost exclusively with the terms of history, in a way that can be extremely interesting and of considerable value, but that can also serve to externalize and alienate. Equating heritage with history can force into a more public and less well connected realm those genuine relationships with the past that have for most of the human experience derived their strength from their more personal, inalienable, and intimate nature. I will argue in this essay that a second sense of heritage, one that I prefer, can be discovered in the details of culture, associated with but not bounded by the past. Culture, I will argue, is more closely and fairly revealing of actual heritage, principally through those primal ideas of inheritance that in subtle and almost invisible ways continue to guide so much of our everyday lives.

Because it is information expressed through daily routines and actions — and generally not put forth or sanctioned by any external authority — the more private, culturally based sense of heritage discussed here can easily be overshadowed by more public expressions of heritage. This dominance can result in the erosion of associations that provide communities with a sense of continuity and birthright. I will address this issue again at the end of this essay, and offer a few suggestions for how we might still nurture these culturally based heritages.

A brief example from Maryland's Eastern Shore should clarify some of these points. One way to recognize heritage is through recounting the history of occupations that are deemed to be of particular significance to an area's identity. In the history of the Eastern Shore, agriculture and fishing industries emerge as particularly worthy of recognition, with some occupational specialties such as those of Chesapeake Bay watermen and waterwomen even reaching iconic status. Museums, exhibits, and festivals extolling these two occupational traditions appear almost everywhere on the Eastern Shore. Increasingly, their celebration is imbued with a strong dose of nostalgia that is derived from real or perceived threats to the survival of Bay fisheries and agriculture. The message is often quite clear. What is at risk here, and what is being memorialized through heritage, is not simply an occupation, but an entire way of life that is associated with that occupation.

This is not an entirely false view, but it is distorted. The distortion lies in having linked through time and geography the lives of people and their communities to a dependency upon very particular kinds of occupations and places. A closer look at cultural heritages associated with many rural Eastern Shore communities reveals a strikingly different set of traditions, in which mobility and adaptability are important parts of their inheritance. Historically, many Eastern Shore families have, of necessity, combined working on the water with other occupations and employments that are generally discounted in reconstructions of their heritage. They have for example, routinely engaged in modest agricultural pursuits, in perennial labor in the markets and industries of Maryland's Western Shore, and participated broadly in the service and trade industries of their own communities. In other words, the labor practices of many Eastern Shore men and women were and still are characterized not so much by dependency upon a single occupation, as they are by an *inherent* resilience which has enabled them to adapt readily to changing economic and environmental conditions.

Which of these views is right — the specific identity (as farmer or waterman) or the innate resilience? In a sense, they are both correct, and the danger lies only in that the first view described has come, often through often repeated heritage representations, to predominate in an assessment of the fate of many rural Chesapeake Bay communities. This view encourages us to consider such communities as bound to traditions associated with very particular ways of earning a living (occupational "traditions" that heritage professionals have helped create for them), and as being without the resources or skill to adapt to changing times. The second view suggests that perhaps the most valuable inheritance shared by many Eastern Shore communities is the resilience and adaptability that has in the past enabled them to survive through hard times, and that will likely serve them in similar fashion well into the future.[2]

The Associations of Heritage

As we tour the Chesapeake Bay, we are likely to discover its heritage as a hodgepodge of sites and places, little oases of historical reference and cultural prominence, representing pieces of a puzzle that will never be completed. Perhaps we can find an analogy in the appearance of many contemporary zoological parks, which are periodically subject to renovation and redesign, but that for reasons of economy can be redone only one small section at a time. Since the theories and practices of exhibiting animals periodically change, different parts of the zoo serve not only to display varied animal species or habitats, but can also be understood to represent different ideas about the relationships of animals to the humans who exhibit and observe them. Though different, this recalls the on-site representation of the Chesapeake Bay region's heritage. Museums, historic houses, nature preserves, festivals, and roadside signs, along with other particulars of place consciousness deemed worthy of recognition, tell us as much about our notions of heritage representation as they tell us about the scenes we pass by and the historical places we stop to visit.

Some historic houses appear as islands in otherwise ordinary small town main streets, and continue to be represented in the heroic, highly romantic ideology of the early 20th century. A museum that documents the Bay area's tobacco heritage struggles in our time to find the most appropriate and fashionable way to represent the social and economic consequences of slavery. Going against the grain, a county planner on Maryland's Western Shore develops a tourist guide to the area's rich religious heritage.[3] An Eastern Shore museum devoted to local fisheries eerily displays the material of commercial fishing with practically no reference to either past or current lives of the fisher folk, while another more recent heritage center dedicated to the same topic is fully integrated into the lives of community members. One way to think of these scattered markers of heritage is to consider them as outposts in a battleground of representation, signifying the struggle to acquire the right or privilege to name a place or object or life way in a particular fashion and to quite specific ends, and thereby, through the protocols of inheritance, to declare a kind of birthright — a bequest that might or might not have been earned by any actual or reasonably intimate past association with such markers.

The word heritage has crept gradually but surely into even the most common vocabularies, emerging over the past couple of decades to a level of such great familiarity that it passes easily into our speech, in a way that nearly convinces us that we know what it means. The word is of course closely related in its origins to the word "inheritance," suggesting a willful and generally private transfer in the ownership of some kind of tangible property from one generation to the next, with a mutual understanding across generations that the property has value. This is interesting because in modern parlance the term heritage becomes public and often problematic and contestable among those who presume to have a stake in its recognition, to include not only direct heirs but interested "outsiders" such as heritage professionals, tourism planners, and developers.

The properties of modern heritage are less transferred than they are transformed in the act of constituting them as heritage. And yet the modern process of heritage recognition transpires most often in the original language of inheritance, implying that the *inherent* value (as opposed, for example, to monetary or investment value) of a piece of heritage has been established in the past and is wholly representative of the sentiments and actions of direct heirs. In reality, the inherent value of modern or public heritage is more accurately acknowledged as an artifact of the present, and is thereby less strictly inherited than it is proclaimed. In this sense, the *assumptions* that underlie most contemporary representations of heritage are closely associated with the idea of inheritance as a kind of birthright, while the *reality* of modern heritage is more contrived and clearly fictive — the stories that our society tells itself.

The idea that our associations with the past result from needs in the present forms the foundation of a good part of current scholarship related to the conceptualization and practical uses of heritage representations. The very requirement of a sense of heritage, or the perception that heritage is something that can be lost and that might have to be saved or preserved, is generally considered to be an artifact of modernity, related in various theoretical renderings to the distancing and alienating effects of industrialization, emergent nationalism, and the concurrent rise of capitalist economies. Well known scholars such as David Lowenthal have argued that the very act of recognizing our past as distinct serves to alter that past in conformity to the political, economic, and cultural needs of the present.[4] Others, such as Eric Hobsbawn and Terence Ranger, have traced the ways in which modern ideologies have become dependent upon the deliberate construction of traditions and heritage markers that serve to reify these ideologies through claims of historical distinction and longevity.[5] For his part, Benedict Anderson has described the mechanisms by which early modern nation states have managed to memorialize and celebrate communal links that are fundamentally fictional but that remain nonetheless compelling and persuasive in the maintenance of our nationalist identities.[6]

These and several other basic critiques have provided the thread for a discussion that has dominated much of the consideration of heritage matters over the past two decades.[7] The relationships of humans to their past began to change with a variety of disruptions associated with industrialization and early modernity.[8] During this period, we witnessed dramatic increases in societal complexity, increased consolidation of power and authority within the nation state, the invention of new and wildly proficient forms of transportation and communication, more efficient ways of producing goods for market, new more tightly controlled and regulated patterns of work and leisure, and a gradual but profound separation of the sacred from the secular.

One readily recognized consequence of these changes has been an abridgement of locality. This has resulted from an erosion of the close associations humans have normally had with particular places, a relationship that dates at least to the origins of settled agricultural communities. With early modernity we see the idea of heritage emerging in a self-conscious way to fill a void created by rapid disruptions of traditional associations with particular places and the ways of organizing human communities that are derived from those associations. These newly designated and already somewhat alienated heritages have served (along with other incentives, which have occasionally included force of arms) to convince previously localized populations to shift their allegiances to more complex world orders — orders which are of a scale that their citizens cannot hope to fully understand or negotiate without assistance. Much of what heritage has been is then transformed, in this long historical moment, from an inheritance to a dependency, in which we all become heirs presumptive to a history that we often cannot even recognize without the prompting of professional guides and keepers of a sometimes crudely and forever partially imagined past.

The heritages of cities and towns of the Chesapeake Bay deemed to be especially revered are often crafted around particular occasions of their history. This practice excludes or trivializes many more links to the past that remain unrecognized. Maryland's capital city of Annapolis, for example, has most typically celebrated its relationship to colonial and 18th century American society. The more clearly localized historic instances and inheritances of the 19th and 20th centuries have figured less prominently in the city's public history, although as we will see later in this essay more recent approaches to Annapolis's public heritage have served to challenge the city's special relationship to a rather exclusive colonial past.

In a similar sense, public heritage tends to focus on those parts of the past that cannot be reached through the remembrances of living people. This is especially true in cases where what is to be represented remains controversial or not fully reconciled in the public conscience. The recent and very partial construction of a publicly acquired African American heritage for the Chesapeake Bay region has, for example, focused on the wrongness of slavery and on the struggle for emancipation, as well as a sporadic recognition of the survival of some African American arts and crafts. Virtually unrecognized are the much more recent histories of post-bellum segregation, discrimination, and violent racial conflict that have characterized much of the region — instances of heritage that remain an important part of the private inheritances of many citizens of the region, and that continue to play important roles in the everyday lives of communities.[9] In a sense, it might be considered that such memories are still so vividly realized that they refuse to yield to a more public interpretation of either their historic significance or their bearing upon the present.

In a localized community, the rules of inheritance are generally well established.[10] Even if they are occasionally challenged, generations still usually seem to enjoy a sense of orderly transition. With the transfer of goods and property within localized communities also comes a fairly disciplined although certainly mutable repossession of identity, and the celebration of identity through inheritance is absolutely linked to a reconfirmation of community. In many modern environs, on the other hand, there has been a disruption in the bridges that link possessions to identity, and hence to a sense of continuity that is invested in both history and culture. Wealth and property are no longer as dependent as they once were upon the kind of cultural routines that, prior to modernity, had served to preserve rules of descent as well as provide a sense of continuity and reliability.

Modernity, it seems, enables us to reinvent our histories and relocate our cultures to meet needs that are clearly associated with the production of wealth and the control of property, but which have lost many of their more "natural" associations with identity and community. How we ultimately come to think of the prospects of heritage, and to regard our own involvement in the appreciation and construction of heritage, depends a great deal upon whether or not we conclude that this modern, large-scale process is inevitable, and therefore bound to eventually eradicate the vital inheritances of more local-ized communities. The eradication of these more private inheritances is a prospect that I find difficult to accept.

To summarize, with modernity we begin to recognize the coexistence of two fairly distinct ways of thinking about and responding to the idea of her-itage. One is mostly cultural (more private), and the other is primarily historical (more public). What I mean by a *cultural* sense of heritage is closely aligned with the idea of a kind of natural inheritance. This habit of natural inheritance is localized and provides the qualities by which human cultures and communities establish those elements of continuity that ensure their dis-tinct survival within a broadly interdependent world. Natural inheritance is often taken for granted by its practitioners, is more tacit than not, and is closely associated with matters of etiquette — which is to say that this cultural sense of heritage finds its meaning in codified, inherited practices that provide guidelines for conduct that permit the maintenance of a group as a localized entity capable of recognizing its own distinction in some meaningful way.[11] This sense of heritage, I suggest, reaches into the begin-nings of human culture and is virtually synonymous with the survival of relatively autonomous human communities (i.e., distinct but not separate cultures).

The other, more public and *historical* sense of heritage is described in fair measure by the kinds of associations with early modernity that I have dis-cussed above. This heritage is more a product of the past couple of centuries, and is most particularly associated with the worldwide rise of national iden-tity and the dominance of industrial capitalism, representing in a very real sense both the commodification and the alienation of heritage from its more localized meanings. It is the conversion of heritage to a matter of primarily historical rather than cultural significance that separates heritage from its immediate and most vital participants — the "real" inheritors in the forms of cultures, communities, and the like — and that facilitates the ability of special interests to control and even define the ways in which representations of heritage are made and proffered.

Authenticity and the Professionalization of Heritage

The heritage "industry" that we recognize today, which has in many respects become synonymous with the idea of heritage itself, is a direct consequence of our attempts to transform heritage from the realm of culturally distinct personal inheritance into a kind of public history. This relatively new way of reflecting upon heritage has required the development of rationales that are intended to make the transformation palatable to its consumers and acceptable to its original heirs. Its importance to the development and maintenance of a distinctly modern consciousness is reflected in good part by the extent to which heritage-as-history has indeed become an industry, with highly segmented yet interdependent parts, invested in criteria of efficiency, control, benefit, and profit, and supported by a wide range of heritage professionals and a vast corps of volunteer workers and interested bystanders.

The early modern professionalization of heritage takes numerous forms and continues well into our time. The processes that have led to this professionalization tend to have some common characteristics. For example, many professional components of the modern heritage industry enjoy somewhat nebulous relationships with the special interests of pre-professional and amateur stakeholders who have independent claims upon particular kinds of heritage resources. An example of the latter from the Chesapeake region would be those community and civic groups which have over generations assumed responsibility for the maintenance of local historic properties that they deem to be important heritage markers. There is also an interesting shift in some cases from the private ownership of declared heritage properties to public ownership or stewardship, as can be seen in the management of many historic properties, and most particularly in the rise of public museums during the 19th century. These incomplete shifts from the private to the public and from amateur to professional stewardship over heritage resources reflect in part the growing relationship between heritage-as-history and modern ideals of universal public education. Here I refer to education in the broadest sense. Heritage has become a means of constructing modern social relationships, by which its practitioners attempt to determine for the public at large what events are to be celebrated, which personages are worthy of honor and emulation, which historic properties and values ought to be preserved, and precisely what it is that we should be learning from the past.

The early modern period has had a profound influence on our conceptualizations of heritage. It is during this period that many current museum and exhibition practices were established, providing clear links between national and regional cultures, progressive ideology, and the realization of the past.[12] In the United States, the last third of the 19th century saw the emergence and institutional development of an historic preservation ethic, broadly supported by the federal government and by local and private interests, and contributing to the professionalization of such areas as historic preservation and archaeology.[13] This same period supported the professional development of field-based and ethnographic pursuits such as folklore studies and cultural anthropology — both fields that had to struggle early on with the concepts of cultural authenticity, history, and the relationships of nations to their diverse constituencies.[14]

While these movements toward the professionalization of heritage occurred primarily in the public sector, and were often associated with institutions of higher education, it is important to recognize that the idea and value of heritage representation was also beginning to be promoted in other places. We can see these values playing a part, for example, in the origin of many regional and local festivals and preservation activities, which have every bit as much to do with the marshaling of civic resources and attracting new business as they have to do with the appreciation of heritage in and of itself. Such practical uses of heritage resources have resonated in the professional training and development of urban and regional planners, architects, and the like. The early modern period also experienced the rapid growth of mass tourism, facilitated by improvements in transportation and communication and often originally structured in relation to heritage-based, nationalistic ambitions. The first mass tourists literally rode to their destination on the engines of trade and commerce, the railroads and freight steamers that served both to transport the raw materials of industry from distant places and to deposit eager and wide-eyed tourists to those same places.[15] The introduction of mass tourism gave rise, of course, to the increased standardization and professional development of a whole range of new industries related to commercial hospitality, tourism planning and development, and transport.

There is another characteristic of the heritage industry that bears mention, and that is the idea of *authenticity*. The movement of heritage resources through processes of modernization is one in which the resource is first removed or alienated from its "natural" or inheritable relationship to the present. It is made into history. In the process, the resource's local, disciplined inheritance value risks becoming diminished, along with any recognition of how the resource might actually relate to the lives of its present heirs.[16] The heritage resource is then brought back into the present as an artifact of the past, to be reassigned as a property of a broader and less intimately connected public, and it is at this point that its authenticity becomes questionable and subject to contestation.

For most of our modern era, the challenge of properly authenticating objects, people and ceremonies that are thought to represent the past has been a matter of considerable importance. This challenge has contributed substantially to the professionalization of the heritage industry, in that many of the newly created professional roles associated with heritage found their early justification in a promise to establish authenticity in seemingly objective and incontestable ways. The new professionals strove to mediate "truths" between the broad, scientific interests of the state and those more clearly personal interests of the original inheritors of particular heritages. To this end, the authority that allowed a modern heritage performance or artifact to be declared real, authentic and, ultimately, as having value, was increasingly invested in persons who viewed any particular heritage context from a distant and outsider perspective.

The criteria of authenticity came to be invested in the presumptions and theories of a variety of professional elites, in which modern scientific inquiry and discourse held precedence over the mythic and presumably naive interpretations of heritage that occurred on a more localized level and from a more intimate and insider perspective. In the early modern period especially, the quest for authenticity often led to disregarding heritage resources that appeared to have been altered from their point of original historical significance. Resources tended to be locked in time, associated with particular historical events or periods, and were primarily valued for their supposed purity or originality in respect to that time. Authenticity was judged in part by the degree to which any heritage resource had managed to evade the contaminations of modern life, in effect denying heritage confirmation to any resource that failed to meet strict and varied criteria of authenticity — criteria, we must keep in mind, that were vested in the rarely challenged assumptions of a variety of heritage professionals.

The struggle for authenticity also introduced the possibility of fakery and inauthenticity in the construction of heritage, rendering entire cultural processes ineligible to be designated as a part of the "real thing." In this context, the concepts of fakery and false representation assumed their importance in relation to a rapid increase in the prestige and monetary value beginning to be associated with authenticity. With increased democratization and the breakdown of more rigid class structures in Europe and North America, the attribution of authenticity provided one of several new standards of taste by which those with the means to do so could further distinguish themselves from the "masses" through the acquisition and display of properly authenticated items and experiences. New wealth filled private homes and museums with authenticized objects of art and craft from around the world, inspired major public preservation efforts, and helped subsidize a travel and tourism industry devoted to the capture of classy, "genuine" experiences. Authenticity became through such practices and venues closely associated with the authority to claim it as such, and the growing ranks of heritage professionals played critical roles in facilitating the new, modern authorization of heritage.

The Disturbances of Heritage

When I first came to live in Maryland, my sense of the Chesapeake Bay had mostly to do with water. The Bay was a place I went to visit and I knew I was there when I could see its water. Later, living in northern Baltimore and out of sight of that city's harbor, I came to know that I was still intimately associated with the Bay, at least through the drainage off my yard. Not long ago, driving up a mountainside in western Pennsylvania, I passed a sign that informed me that I had, some 200 miles away and well out of sight of the Bay, just reached a western limit of the Chesapeake Bay drainage system.

My point is simple enough. How we experience a place like the Bay varies considerably depending upon the particular point of view we take or are encouraged to take. These shifting viewpoints occur not only to us as individuals, but in some sense also occur culturally, where I believe our collective sense of the Bay has been ever so subtly shifting from a notion of the Chesapeake Bay as "country," connoting a well defined and familiar landscape, slow to change, mostly pacific and primarily rural in its nature, to an idea of the Chesapeake Bay as "region," which suggests a somewhat less familiar and rather amorphous place, less approachable on a human scale, more restive and urban in its reach.

Associated with this shift is a tendency to begin to see the Bay as much for what we bring to it and put in it as for what we take from it, and more as a system to be managed in a consistent and predictable way (i.e., a thoroughly "modern" way), and less as an experience of place to be valued on the basis of hard-earned and distinctly local associations. Our perspectives of the Chesapeake Bay have begun to drift from considerations of its nature and integrity to an interest in its reach and impact, and from a relationship to the Bay that has been based primarily on associations (the relationships of people) to one that is based on systems (the relationships of organisms [i.e., ecosystems] and objects).

This shift is in keeping with much of what I describe in this essay. We have been experiencing for some time a major transformation from the local and personal to a more readily depersonalized and bureaucratized sense of the "public." And yet we have acquired by far the greater part of our feelings of responsibility for the world in which we live through local and personal associations, and the obligations that attend our most direct and meaningful inheritances. It remains an open question whether we can be as responsible as we need to be in any other way, without these local attachments.

The heritage inventions of the early modern age were in many respects shaped by a struggle to describe and celebrate not local but national destinies. They embodied ambitions related to the future as much as they reflected the aims of the present or accurately represented any known past. In this respect, these inventions at least aspired to be inheritances, in much the same way as heritage might have been represented and lived through prior to the advent of modern nation states, but with an important difference. The intricacies of inheritance associated with locality and community were beginning to be subsumed by a larger and eventually much less accessible sense of heritage. As a result, it became necessary to invent some new routine through which participation in this sense of heritage could be assured. It is not an easy thing to convince people who might not even recognize each other's existence to form common purpose with a state.

To buy into the idea of a common heritage, and the mutual aspirations that this commonality might indicate, there had to be at least a glimmer of hope that all the members of the state might aspire to that heritage — an implied promise that, in terms of inheritance, the state might indeed become the *estate* of its constituencies. And this is the essence of early modern transformations of heritage, many of which still hold fast in our consciousness. In this respect, the effective influence of the state can vary considerably. Along the Chesapeake Bay, for example, the Western Shore and tidewater region are clearly associated with the founding of the United States, but on much of the Eastern Shore of Maryland and Virginia, heritage remains more clearly localized and in some cases resistant of the dominant story. Not withstanding a few places such as Kent County's Washington College, few on Maryland's Eastern Shore seem to pay much attention to where any "founding fathers" might have visited or spent the night. Many continue to take pride in the maverick associations that inform much of the region's coastal heritage, replete with instances of piracy, religious autonomy, Confederate sympathies, poaching, and other occasions of resistance to state authority.

Over the past couple of decades, we have begun to witness significant transformations in the way heritage concepts are being employed. While earlier conceptualizations of heritage often helped serve the interests of national identity through the creation of mainstream national *histories*, many more recent conceptualizations of heritage tend toward recognizing those groups and occasions which have been excluded from the mainstream, or at least gone unrecognized in an effort to emphasize common purpose and broadly shared experience.

It is also worth recognizing that the professionalization of heritage that began during the early modern period has provided much of the structure for subsequent "disruptions" of heritage discussed below. For the most part, the same institutions that were constructed to serve the interests of a nationalized, historically focused sense of heritage are now at the forefront of the late-modern challenges to that version of heritage making. What we need to keep in mind is that however well-intentioned, insightful, and potentially useful these recent professional and scholarly critiques might be, they still do limit the possibilities for a re-conceptualization of modern heritage, in that they tend to assume the need for institutional mediation between heritage and its subjects. I will have occasion in the final part of this essay to question whether this presumed need for mediation, which is itself a product of modern heritage conceptualization, is actually a necessary precondition for the revelation of meaningful cultural heritage and inheritance.

Re-Presented Heritage(s)

One function of modern heritage is to memorialize. The trend of the past two decades or so has not challenged this role as much as it has attempted to make a shift from the often dominant assumptions of earlier representations to a more relativistic, diverse, and "popular" sense of determining what is worth being remembered. New emphases on heritage recognition within the United States have focused particularly on memorializing the pasts of ethnic minorities, specific working class populations, and of women. While earlier representations of these marginalized groups tended to place them within the context of customary and traditional practices, often emphasizing the unique or quaint and decidedly non-ordinary aspects of their lifestyles, recent representations more often situate such groups within contexts of social class discrimination, racism, and economic exploitation.

The lesson here is that heritage representation invariably serves particular purposes, and when new purposes are needed then new heritages have to be brought to the mix. In regard to Annapolis, Maryland, one scholar has suggested that the city's notable transience (having been both a commercial and recreational seaport as well as the place for regional government) has deprived it of any readily identifiable "essence."[17] Parker B. Potter argues that the local elite focused upon and in some respects invented Annapolis's colonial past in order to maintain a separation between themselves and the city's many maritime, tourist, and political visitors and institutions. By limiting the celebration of its past to the history of an elite, white citizenry, the city also helped determine the kinds of visitors who would be most likely to feel comfortable in Annapolis. This deliberate creation of Annapolis's past not only, he argues, served the purposes of separation and distinction, but also helped to attract even more visitors (of the right kind) to the city.

The singular sense of heritage that appears to have served Annapolis well into the first half of the 20th century has been reshaped over the past several decades in response to some of the shifts in heritage re-presentation described above. A major impetus to this change has been the work of University of Maryland professor Mark Leone and his colleagues, in the founding of the "Archaeology in Annapolis" program. Archaeology in Annapolis was established during the 1980s as a means of using archaeological investigation to reveal the consequences of class and inequality in early Annapolis, and as well to reflect on its own relationship to the city's present and to resist being absorbed by those elite institutions which have characteristically prevailed in Annapolis.[18] To this end, the program was devoted to a "public archaeology," in which the craft of archaeology and its interpretation were made transparent and accessible to the city's public by inviting visitors to tour excavation sites and other forms of outreach. Along with this more reflexive approach to heritage interpretation, the subjects of Annapolis's newly emerging heritage changed dramatically with the advent of the Archaeology in Annapolis program, with primary attention paid to the previously neglected history of the city's non-elite citizenry,[19] to the African American presence in Annapolis,[20] as well as to the historical under-representation of women in colonial Annapolis.[21]

The re-presentation of heritage is closely linked to the increased popularity of an emergent "social history" that tends more to chastise than to celebrate the past. Such heritage representations aim to amend the historical record in significant and usually very particular ways. If the emphasis of earlier modes of heritage presentation rested with identifying those characteristics (i.e., character-defining moments) of the past that contributed to the progressive development of a nation or a people, the primary aim of the new social history has been to describe how particular groups of people have been victimized by the past. While the earlier approach recognizes diversity and cultural difference within a larger presumption of common cultural goals, the new social history focuses on disparate goals and inherent conflicts. One problem here is that there often seems to be nowhere to go from these particularized representations of such practices as slavery, ethnic and class conflict, and gender inequity. There is no clear prospect, no envisioning of a less divisive or less cynical future, for in surrendering the celebratory and progressive nature of an earlier sense of heritage we seem also to have at least momentarily misplaced the possibilities of a more deeply valued tomorrow.

The struggle to re-present heritage and to set the historical record straight has been accompanied by a set of attitudes related to "new" ways that heritage might now be discovered, presented, and rationalized as a benefit to those whose heritage comes to be represented. Some have argued that the recovery of heritage should be engaged through participatory processes that are meant to involve persons and descendent communities in the discovery and interpretation of their particular heritages. It is often presumed that such efforts might also serve to "empower" such people, although the route to such a lofty if slightly paternalistic goal is generally speculative and vague, and its realization is rarely tested.[22]

In their study of Colonial Williamsburg's well known living history museum, Richard Handler and Eric Gable[23] have suggested that the promise of the new social history to accurately represent, debate, and hopefully reconcile diverse heritages is compromised by the heritage professionals' dependence on an institutional structure that remains accountable to sponsors and visitors who seek a more celebratory history of the past. In a similar manner, Barbara Kirshenblatt-Gimlett[24] has discussed the ways in which vested interests, occupational exigencies, and disciplinary priorities continue to shape the re-presentations of heritage by museum and folklore professionals.[25]

Recent attempts to uncover and publicly present African American heritage at a place like Colonial Williamsburg serve to demonstrate how subtly heritage constructions can serve a variety of intentions and ideologies.[26] Despite well-intended efforts to be more inclusive and "multi-cultural" in their presentation of the African American experience in Colonial Williamsburg, there remains a disparity between how white and black heritages are routinely interpreted. Presentations of white history and culture (focused on the nation's founding fathers) tend to be offered as factual and incontestable. One the other hand, the presentations of black history and culture are more conjectural and relativistic, and in this light their "truth" is perhaps less convincing. The authors of this very interesting study also question the way Colonial Williamsburg's curators represent the material cultures of both whites and blacks. In these instances, material is attributed on the basis of ownership, and since few blacks owned much at the time, their material culture is represented as negligible and limited to a few utilitarian items. The authors point out that a different choice in how to represent material culture would provide us with a much different sense of African American heritage. If the attributions of material culture were made on the basis of use rather than ownership, the material culture of colonial Williamsburg's African Americans would appear much richer, since black slaves regularly used the property of their owners, if only in service to them.

Places and a Sense of Culture

The early modern development of heritage was founded on a close association of places and cultures. For example, ethnographic museum displays generally focused on distinct geographies, to the extent that place and cultural identity seemed almost synonymous. Cultural distinction itself tended to depend on a celebration of place and isolation. In this scenario, one justification for memorializing the past is a belief that distinct cultures and their unique places are indeed *dying*, often as a result of the spread of modern institutions and industries and their somewhat amorphous cultural styles. In response to such threats of cultural genocide, museums and other heritage locations have often served as closets in which the ghostly pieces of rapidly disintegrating and disappearing life-ways might be stored, in part as curiosities, but also in some ambiguous way as lessons from the past, or conversely as monuments of conquest. There is not a little collective hubris associated with these memorializations, constructed as they are upon a premise that some kinds of cultures die, their places ruined, in effect becoming de-authenticated or made artificial. While feared and occasionally despised even by their major beneficiaries, modern landscapes, with their sprawling tendency toward sameness and even global domination, are also imbued with a certain superiority and a powerful ability to transform and continually reinvent their cultures. Meanwhile, other presumably less dynamic cultures and communities seem destined to become only heritage.

Early conceptualizations of culture and its places provided the basis for what some scholars now criticize as an "essentialist" notion of cultural difference. Here the idea of cultural distinction assumes characteristics that are often (and wrongly) associated with racial concepts — the myth of homogeny in premodern cultures, the vulnerability of "weaker" or presumably less dynamic belief systems, and pronounced distinctions between people of different places, ethnicities, and "character." These essentialist ideas have often been used to at least imply that some cultures (specifically, modern, Western, and scientific rationalist cultures) have the capacity to be dynamic and hence progressive cultural forces, while others (more often traditional, isolated, superstitious places) are more or less static and not likely to survive significant threats to their ways of life or belief systems.

But the ideas of culture and its places are changing. We have begun to recognize that distinction, as described below, can be as much a contributor to the maintenance and celebration of cultural diversity as isolation might sometimes have been. In this sense, distinction simply refers to ways in which groups emphasize their unique collective identities as a result of contact with others, rather than as a result of being isolated from others. In other words, processes of cultural differentiation are alive and well, although the means by which contemporary cultural distinctions are being made are not well understood. This challenges the long held sense that cultural diversity is invariably a product of the isolation and remoteness of human populations, rather than a result of their purposefully constructing and maintaining unique cultural identities within a context of regular and often intense cultural exchange.

Such differences in the styles of heritage presentation can easily be located around the Chesapeake Bay. In Crisfield, Maryland, for example, a town noted for its association with the economically and symbolically important blue crab fishery, the J. Millard Tawes Historical Museum focuses on the craft and tools of the fishery and presents them more as distant artifacts than as objects which have a continuity that stretches into the present. At the end of a short boat trip from Crisfield, the more recently constructed Smith Island Center is about pretty much the same things as the Tawes museum, but to a much different effect. The award-winning design of the Smith Island Center was intended to serve as a meeting place for Smith Islanders as well as to accommodate the interests of tourists. This dual purpose has lent vitality to the presentation of Smith Island heritage, providing a place in which public presentation can coexist with activities that serve to reinforce local associations and relationships. In effect, the center recognizes and to some extent facilitates the confluence of different cultural traditions, rather than inadvertently constructing a wall between them.

When we accept the capacity of cultures to differentiate as a result of routine and intimate associations with other cultural traditions, we also see the places that are associated with culture being transformed and rethought. The kinds of representations of heritage that might be found in museums and celebratory spaces or at typical heritage events are clearly beginning to change. One such change, as noted above in respect to the Smith Island Center, is an increased appreciation of the dynamic nature of all cultural inheritances. More recent representations of heritage have become less dependent on establishing specific places where the occurrence of some kind of inheritance is thought to have occurred. We are beginning to understand how well heritage travels, and to search out its occurrences in such locales and processes as immigrant and expatriate communities, refugee camps, and even through the Internet. For example, a recent effort to chronicle the varied folk life of the Delmarva peninsula[27] included as a major part of its research a comprehensive survey of the peninsula's relatively recently established Latino population — an inclusive approach to uncovering local heritage that would have been unlikely even a decade ago.[28]

Increased understanding of how Chesapeake Bay communities have formed into seemingly distinct heritages reveals considerably less social and economic isolation than has often been imagined, with a significant amount of movement between shore communities and major urban centers such as Annapolis and Baltimore. These movements include seasonal and permanent migration among watermen communities and the influence of Chesapeake Bay tourists and visitors.[29] Because of such movements and interactions, Chesapeake Bay maritime communities seem less like specific geographical presences, and more like sets of common relationships and cultural exchanges among widely dispersed groups of people — people engaged in a variety of

occupations and associated with different places. Cultural heritage and inheritance have not so much a center as discernible routes by which they travel. A
more mobile sense of heritage helps to reshape our ideas of how both culture
and historical memory work. Where earlier styles of cultural representation
carried the presumption of high degrees of homogeneity in belief and value,
it is now possible to imagine cultural processes that are *in their normal state*
highly susceptible to dissolution and disruption, continual renegotiation,
manipulation, and re-imagining. The idea of preserving a culture free of the
forces of change and modification seems never to have been tenable, and the
notion of such a static community likely runs counter to the most vital cultural processes by which societies have always maintained themselves.

Our confidence in the ability of defined and delimited places to contain
culture and represent heritage has eroded in part as a result of increased globalization and the expansion of capitalist markets into heritage and tourism
"products."[30] A second manifestation of the fading of an essentialist and more
static idea of culture and heritage has appeared in the recent tendency to recognize spaces and places in a broader context, enabling us to better represent
the melding and negotiation of heritage traditions within larger contexts and
over time. There has, for example, been increased interest in recognizing and
preserving heritage "landscapes," not so much as terrains bound to particular
historical eras or events, but as exemplars of the processes through which relationships between human communities and their environments are worked
out over time.[31]

A more mobile approach to heritage recognition is also embodied in the
increased popularity of attempts to regionalize (rather than "special"-ize) heritage places through the creation of heritage trails, networks, waterways,
routes, and varied other paths and gateways. The formative and tentative
nature of many of these endeavors is often apparent. For example, the
National Park Service's recent declaration of a heritage initiative that celebrates "gateways" to the Chesapeake Bay has progressed in such a way as to
identify multiple points of entrance (hence, the "gateways") to a sense of heritage that itself seems bodiless and undefined. The entrances have in this
instance, at least for the time being, become the primary objects of representation. That such an approach should be compatible with a transformation
from a sense of heritage that is dependent upon establishing authenticity to a
new means of heritage identification that simply assigns varied measures of
significance to heritage objects and events seems quite obvious — our sense of

heritage locations are becoming more fluid and transitory in part because we find it increasingly difficult to discern from the actual objects of heritage any sense of primary custom, belief, or practice.[32]

As much as recent trends in heritage representation have indicated a tendency to disassociate culture from the specificity of place, the continued importance of establishing some sense of locality is difficult to deny, although the "placeness" of place in our time can be difficult to discern. Some scholars have recognized that recent trends toward increased globalization may well serve as a challenge to the survival of nation states as they have been conceived, even though globalization remains dependent in other ways upon a strong sense of place — as we find presented in Arif Dirlik's discussion of the need to temper the effects of worldwide dislocations with renewed forms of "place-based consciousness,"[33] or Arjun Appadurai's introduction of the concept of "diasporic public spheres" as harbingers of new and highly mobile, shifting, refreshingly heterogeneous "localities."[34]

In other words, it seems possible that the ideas of place and locality are themselves being reinvented in response to the rapid disruptions and relocations of our time. This adaptability no doubt results in part from the increased capability of new information technologies to rupture expected relationships between locality and location. In a sense this enables heritages to be reconstituted, relatively free of the constraints of geographic obstacles and national boundaries. New places can therefore be ethereally established as constructions of ever greater convenience. Optimistically, such a tendency might serve in the case of a place like the Chesapeake Bay to begin to prevail against the transition from "country" to "region" that I alluded to earlier, with the potential to create new and viable spaces in such a way as to reinsert the familiarity and human scale of the country into the more amorphous and impartial specter of a region.

Ecologies of Hope and Descent

Early modernist ideas about relationships between human endeavor and the natural environment tended to focus in near equal parts upon a broadly accepted need to conquer unruly (i.e., nonrational) nature and the promotion of a sense of environmental stewardship. That stewardship originally emphasized ensuring a dependable supply of natural resources to meet the expanding needs of a rapidly industrializing society. In the United States, the first clear wave of expansionist/conservationist sentiment became apparent during Theodore Roosevelt's presidency, with the promotion of a highly rationalized approach to multiple-purpose natural resource development. Here, separations between humanity and nature were clear, with little doubt as to which part of the equation should exist in service to the other. The needs of civilization had in this optimistic and expansive era clearly risen above those of any sense of nature that might be held to be independent of human ambition. Culturally speaking, the only people of this era who might be imagined to enjoy close and reasonably equitable relationships with the *natural* environment were those "primitive" groups that progress had already left behind. By the turn of the 20th century the idea that humans might live in harmony with nature had itself become a notion associated with the past — an idea that, for example, figured prominently in the increasingly romanticized way that pre-contact aboriginal cultures were represented in museums and various displays, although there was scant evidence that such natural harmonies had truly existed even then.

In our time, representations of nature seem less clear, although also generally more appreciative of the limits and ecological dangers of unrestrained economic expansion. One major trend declares nature and the environment part of human heritage. Another, just making its way onto the stage, attempts to make culture work more like we imagine nature to work, in effect refashioning heritage in relation to an ecological dynamic.[35] Accompanying both these trends is a growing ecological movement that shifts our attention from an equilibrium model emphasizing the inherent balance of the environment to a greater appreciation for imbalances and dynamic influences now recognized as intrinsic features of environmental systems. This fluid model is itself effected in part by the perceived inseparability of human and natural processes.[36]

The first trend, often posited in terms of some kind of "environmental heritage," has progressed rapidly over the past decade, serving in part as an attempt to link cultural practices to the goals of environmental conservation and preservation. Such practices might include the appreciation of historic associations with natural landmarks, aesthetic and symbolic values associated with natural objects and environments, as well as culturally constructed ideals related to concepts of wilderness and to "pristine" qualities of nature.[37] Such conceptualizations serve to bring nature into the heritage camp, and to make the *natural* subject to some of the same problems associated with the identification and management of other heritage resources. For example, if natural features and places are to be protected and preserved for their heritage value, then whose natural heritage shall we represent?

While some specific environmental heritage features might be broadly valued and seem fairly innocuous, such as the famed and unfortunately lost Wye Oak of Maryland's Eastern Shore, many if not most natural environments and ecosystems are subject to existing and competitive patterns of resource appreciation and exploitation. If, for example, agriculture, fisheries, forestry, and even regional tourism development are all associated in their respective ways with the "natural" heritage of the Chesapeake Bay region, with each of these industries being representative of distinct and often competing human-environmental relationships, then which do we favor as we seek to solve any of the Bay's recognized environmental problems? The answer that we should favor those practices that are most beneficial or least harmful to the environment no longer works, because by linking the environment to human heritage we have in effect put multiple environments in place, each associated in different ways to the human experience, and each *legitimately* capable of providing quite different solutions to any environmental problem.

One of the dangers of claiming the environment as a part of human heritage lies in the temptation to then assume a close parallel between the ways in which human social systems and environmental systems work. This tendency can be seen clearly, for example, in many current criteria established for determining the sustainability of ecosystems, which tend to link principles of environmental conservation with broadly secular and thoroughly "Western" tenets of participatory and democratic environmental decision making.

It is not at all clear that principles or practices indicative of sustainable natural systems apply equally well or in the same way to the maintenance of proximate social and cultural systems. Though we would like to imagine that there is a certain amount of integrity between natural and cultural systems, there is little solid evidence to suggest that this is or is not the actual case.

To the extent that we might agree upon comparable indicators of sustainability across the lines of natural and cultural systems, these indicators still seem to take on interesting if not confounding lives of their own. Take, for example, the principle of diversity. The values associated with diversity figure prominently in declarations of sustainability related to both natural systems (i.e., species and biotic diversity) and cultural systems (i.e., multicultulturalism, respect for democratic principles, and equity across ethnic, class, and gender lines). The question here is to determine the extent to which such principles are actually compatible enough to contribute to the making of sound resource management policy. In *The Ecology of Hope*, Ted Bernard and Jora Young assume that there is little conflict between principles of natural and cultural diversity, and they base their call for social and ecologically sound sustainable development on these assumptions of compatibility.[38] On the other hand, the environmental historian Donald Worster has noted how little we actually do understand about the interactions of cultural and natural systems, and has at least hinted that those human communities that have best managed to sustain the health and diversity of their natural environments over long periods of time might well be those that are less culturally diverse in their own right, and more likely to value social responsibility to the community as a whole over the exercise of individual or minority rights — communities that are, in other words, rather conservative and perhaps quite dogmatic in their nature, resistant to the intrusions of "outsiders."[39]

The local tenets of environmental conservation to which Worster alludes are likely to be embedded in the natural inheritances of communities. If we consider again Chesapeake Bay watermen and women and their communities, this time from the standpoint of natural resource conservation, we might find some interesting insights based on this idea of inheritances. David Griffith[40] and Michael Paolisso[41] have both provided models related to how watermen make decisions about resource conservation. For Paolisso, such decisions are invested in a basic right to work the water that figures prominently in the watermen's natural inheritance. Griffith comes to similar conclusions regarding the watermen's relationship to nature as a kind of gift relationship based on fairly strict principles of reciprocity. These tried and true relationships to the resources upon which watermen depend seemed to work well enough until demand for the resource intensified, and pollution and other environmental factors began to signal an end to the days of seemingly limitless harvest. With these new pressures, state control of natural resources has developed in much the same way as we have considered the appropriation of cultural heritage — in other words, the state comes to represent an intangible and dislocated "public right" to the resource that presumes to supercede earlier, local inheritances upon which watermen communities had built a culture. With intensified resource competition, the advent of some kind of public ethic is probably inevitable. What is not inevitable, however, is the prospect that such an ethic should be expected to effectively replace the more intimate associations and expectations that have long governed the watermen's relationship to their environment. As we have seen in regard to cultural heritage, obligations toward and responsibilities for environmental heritage are most effectively realized through local inheritances.[42]

The Craftings of Leisure and Tourism

Many of the trends discussed previously in this section point toward a liberalization of heritage, with at least a hint that the properties of inheritance were somehow usurped during the early modern period and that they ought now be returned to their rightful heirs — although exactly who those heirs might now be, or what it really is that needs to be returned, remains highly contestable.[43] At the same time, we have seen that many of the heritage structures and practices associated with the early modern period have managed to survive these liberating influences. We have, for example, noted this to be the case in regard to professions associated with heritage research and with the development and management of heritage resources, as well as with the institutions that house these professions and continue to serve as the primary repositories of heritage. In a sense, everything is different, and yet very little has changed.

It is possible that this movement toward a more inclusive public sense of heritage might have progressed more fully and with greater speed were it not for one other fairly recent trend, in which heritage has come to enjoy considerable commodity value. This value is realized in large part through efforts to develop and market natural and cultural heritage as tourism opportunities. Although some degree of heritage tourism has long been associated with leisure travel, the manufacture of heritage in the shape of tourism locations has never had so great an influence on how people and their places are represented as it does now. Tourism has become a major world industry. It is not only of vital economic importance to many parts of the globe, including the Chesapeake Bay region, but it is also becoming the lens through which we imagine into being our relationships to each other, to our environment, and to particular heritages. To these ends, inheritances are further complicated and potentially alienated from their rightful heirs as their importance to tourism increases in respect to both the commodity and representational values of heritage. Many of the current social, environmental, and political struggles associated with the Chesapeake Bay region are directly related to a gradual but sure re-imagining of many areas of the Bay from places of work and industry to places of leisure and recreation.

Of course, tourism is not a singular activity, with easily predictable results, although its theorists often treat it as such. There are varieties of tourism as well as varied conditions in which touristic activities occur. If there is any effect of tourism that can be generalized, it may well be the claim that it has come to play an important if not vital role in the ways in which places and people come to be known to the rest of the world. How such representations and knowledge are made, and to what particular ends, speaks directly to the relationships between tourism and heritage. An example can be taken from recent historical changes in the ways in which people tour parts of the Chesapeake region.

The Bay has known tourism for some time, claiming Captain John Smith as one its first nonindigenous visitors. But the first major wave of organized or "mass" tourism to Chesapeake and Delmarva locations began in the mid-1880s, and was focused largely on Chesapeake Bay beach resorts and the newly developing Atlantic coastal towns, particularly Ocean City. A second and distinct surge in organized tourism began during the 1950s, with the construction of the first Chesapeake Bay bridge, linking the Delmarva peninsula to the Washington D.C. and Baltimore metropolitan corridor. This latter period also coincides with an outward expansion of suburban development in Maryland and Virginia, resulting in larger numbers of people moving to places on the two states' western shores, and also with heightened interest in recreational sailing on the Chesapeake Bay. These two quite different types of tourism contribute, along with other influences, to what I described earlier as a transition from a view of Chesapeake Bay locales as having an association with *country* to a more recent view that tends to regard the Bay as *region* — the former being differently epitomized and eulogized in such books as Tom Horton's *Bay Country* (1987), William Warner's *Beautiful Swimmers* (1976), and William Turner's *East of the Chesapeake* (1998), and the latter realized largely in the documents of planners and resource managers and the hopelessly generic tone of most tourism promotions.

Early mass tourism to the Bay, starting during the 19th century, had several interesting characteristics. It exercised a kind of leisure that at the time was a privilege of class, so there was for the most part a clear distinction between the tourist and the toured (although numerous locals did during the time acquire considerable wealth and an elevation of their social position as a result of their involvement in tourism). Another characteristic was that many visitors appear to have had a genuine interest in local customs and objects and an appreciation for the qualities of the places they visited. This was a form of tourism that appears to have been more intimately associated with local life than the tourism that was to follow.

Beach resorts were built alongside and in association with commercial fishing activities. Tourists took advantage of unrehearsed opportunities to observe locals at their labor. They arrived by relatively difficult means on steamships and railways, and often traveled with the goods, particularly the agricultural and fishery products, of the region. The food they enjoyed in their resorts sprang from local products and cuisines — "country cooking" for a largely urban guest population. Except, perhaps, for the food, the opportunities for contact with local heritage was not explicitly staged for tourist consumption. Popular descriptions of the Chesapeake and its environs by visitors, found in the literary and news magazines of the day, include accounts of the gracious if sometimes naive hospitality of local tourism workers, the hard existence of subsistence farmers and watermen, the folkloric customs of the region's African American population, and the waning but still impressive gentility of the area's elite plantation economy.

In other words, tourism of this time had a close association with the places in which it occurred. There appear to have been few conflicts between the needs of visitors and the industries or ambitions of the local population. Tourism seemed compatible with and able to celebrate the region's country nature, combining leisure and privilege with an appreciation for the differences between the demands of a challenging urban existence and a somewhat idealized rural life. This is not to say that this style of tourism did not also serve up distorted, highly romanticized, or sometimes quite negative images of the local population, or that tourism development did not on occasion disadvantage existing Chesapeake Bay communities. Still, these moments seemed to have been relatively rare and in some ways quite innocent, at least in comparison with what was to follow.

The second stage of tourism development, associated with the opening of the Chesapeake Bay bridge and other factors, represents to my mind the urbanization of the region. It is also indicative of a kind of democratization of tourism, with increasing numbers of people having the means and opportunity to travel and enjoy leisure activities. Interestingly enough, this democratization, which in effect has served to reduce class and income disparities between Chesapeake tourists and their "hosts," seems to have led to increased conflict rather than greater compatibility between the two groups. In part, this may be because the earlier form of tourism maintained a fairly clear standard of taste and decorum, a distinct tourism aesthetic, that actually served many of the interests of both hosts and guests. Now, with less incentive to maintain class-oriented etiquettes associated with the earlier tourism, a major source of conflict is found in local complaints about the behaviors of tourists — behaviors that, in essence, seem to be just too pedestrian and lacking in gentility. While 19th century tourists to the Bay and its environs were seeking temporary refuge from the city, most contemporary visitors and the myriad facilities and industries that support their tourisms seem much more likely to bring the city and its ways with them, showing disregard if not disdain for the more settled lives through which they pass.

The modes of transportation associated with various stages of tourism development are important here. When earlier tourists traveled to places like the Delmarva peninsula by steamship and rail, they visited ports and stations of commerce as important places and, as I mentioned above, the goods of the region accompanied them on their journeys. By rail, travel was often intimate, passing through rather than around settlements and providing unguarded glimpses into the backyards and working places of communities. In the second stage of tourism, the two major forms of transportation to and through the region are the automobile and the privately owned sailboat or motorboat. Automobiles remove people from local commerce and from having much knowledge of it — their efficiencies tend to support the rise of generic fast food places and chain motels that grow on the fringes of towns. Private boats reduce the need for many local hospitality services, usually provide for little contact with locals, and in some cases lead to serious competition between tourists and locals for waterfront access.[44]

Destinations are equally significant, and it is important to note that the second wave of tourism development has increasingly taken the form of second home and/or condominium developments and retirement communities. These represent a type of tourism where associations between hosts and guests are altered, obscured, and in some respects greatly reduced, and where the tourist has now entered into a property relationship with his or her tourism site. Property, of course, can have dramatic impacts on the aesthetics of place. New visitor-residents may no longer appreciate local characteristics

and customary associations — such as work locales, certain agricultural pursuits, favorite meeting places, and even the appearance of local residences —
if these appear to impact property values, or to affect new, more leisured uses
of public and private spaces. In this way, evidence of local industry, such as
working watermen's craft and tools, may be "zoned" out of sight, to be
replaced by more pleasing and easily controlled miniaturizations and replicas
of maritime craft and sea creatures that are made to adorn mailboxes and
front yards. In similar fashion, a local bar or café might be transformed into
an upscale cocktail lounge or expensive restaurant, appealing to visitors and
newcomers, but leaving something of a hole in the daily lives of longer-term
residents.

While the earlier tourism to the Chesapeake Bay introduced the country to
denizens of the city, in ways that seem fairly interesting, conservative, and reasonably benign, although also somewhat exclusive, the present shape of
tourism is part of a process that brings the city and its ways of ordering and
valuing things to the country — and here, in this process, what is lost is not so
much in the economic realm, as a loss of livelihood, but is rather the loss of an
aesthetic of association that can help make any particular way of life seem
worthwhile. What is in jeopardy are the valuable and worthwhile distinctions
between giving and receiving genuine hospitality, the loss of neighbors and
the acquisition of people who live next-door, and, perhaps most important of
all, the loss of the power of associations which enable people to determine for
themselves the needs and aspirations of the communities in which they have
lived. Such losses in the Chesapeake Bay region are easily documented and,
unfortunately, increasingly common.[45]

The transition in tourism practices to which I have alluded is far from over
and far from complete. As I have noted elsewhere, recent tourism activities
and attitudes seem to expand upon rather than replace earlier modes of
tourism. The increased popularity of often site-specific heritage tourism
seems almost an anachronism when one considers that modern forms of
tourism and visitation rely so heavily on the provision of familiar and predictable touristic experiences, such as can be provided by fast food eateries,
chain motels, generic marinas, and high rise condominiums. The danger, of
course, is that even place-based heritage representations might become just as
predictable and easily read. This danger is already apparent in much new heritage tourism, which — while it may avoid the more nationalistic representations of early modernism and favor messages that pertain to multivocality,

diversity, and an appreciation of complex cultural processes — also tends to accomplish this in a cookie cutter fashion. In other words, the local actors and scenery of heritage tourism sites might change from place to place, but the message is likely to remain pretty much the same, resulting in representations that celebrate difference, attempt to relegate inequalities to the past, and sanitize conflict. Such representations may incorrectly assume universal and equal participation in the expression of intangibles such as diversity, secular democracy, tolerance, and environmental stewardship.

From Authenticity to Significance

The transformations of heritage discussed above suggest among other things a movement from the certainty of the early modern period, in which heritage tended to assume a pattern of righteously assumed class and cultural leadership (or domination, if we prefer), to a much less certain period in which the property *rights* associated with specific heritages have become contestable while the property *values* to be realized through heritage representations have dramatically raised the stakes associated with heritage claims. Although these recent shifts have encouraged the ideal of attempting to return heritage to its rightful heirs, the actual process is complicated by the fact that the purveyors of heritage are pretty much the same as they have been in the past, and representations of heritage still tend to favor the strictly historical over the processes of cultural inheritance. The increased value of heritage resources, realized through such activities as tourism and community development, has also helped militate against surrendering state or commercial control over the ways in which heritage can be designated and developed as an attractive, place-defining, and economically rewarding resource.

Still, disruptions of the kind noted above have led to new ways of valuing and apportioning heritage resources. There has been a major shift from the idea that *authenticity* is the prime measure of the worth of a heritage representation to the idea that heritage is better evaluated and presented in relation to its *significance* to specific people or relevant stakeholder groups. In other words, the meanings associated with heritage objects and places have loosened up and become more broadly negotiable. Recent heritage designations are often subject to a wider range of partisan beliefs (or if we prefer, stakeholder positions) that serve in some instances to challenge the roles traditionally played by heritage professionals, whose expert testimony and judgment has generally served a more decisive and exclusive part in determining absolute heritage value, but who are increasingly encouraged to share their authority with the more personalized testimonies of a wider variety of stakeholders and parties of interest. This gradual and very incomplete change has begun to produce not only a new measure of truth (or now *truths*) of heritage interpretations, but in many respects also a new aesthetic of heritage appreciation in which things that seem the antithesis of heritage — for example, the vinyl siding of a home — might in certain conditions become imbued with historical significance and appreciative value.[46] Context has become more important than time in discovering heritage, and an appreciation for the processes associated with heritage making has begun to replace a more static and singular view of heritage resources.

The recognized and much sought after tourism potential of places like the Chesapeake Bay contributes in its own right to new measures of significance as some communities struggle to recognize their own heritage potential in relation to the possible interests of outsiders. One manifestation has involved making tourism and recreation its own object of heritage interest, through renewed interest in the Bay's long association with recreational hunting[47] and in recent attempts to reconstitute now defunct resorts and amusement parks of Western and Eastern Shores into heritage tourism sites.[48]

While the idea of significance might raise our hopes in terms of encouraging greater local participation in heritage matters, because it tends to increase the value of local heritage interpretations and to make more transparent the entire business of valuing heritage, for reasons discussed above we must still be wary of the extent to which current promotions of heritage actually provide opportunities for the expression of more "natural" and privately realized inheritance rights and obligations associated with heritage claims.

Our earlier consideration of change in the character of Chesapeake Bay tourism helps to elucidate this argument. Early (mid-19th century), tourism to the region was clearly based on elite standards, and the relative absence of conflict between the tourist and the toured can be attributed in great part to the observation that these standards were valued even by those who did not have the economic means to attain them. These individuals were still often the willing participants and aspirants to a heritage-laden "American Dream" in which endeavor and ambition might prevail over birthright. The shift in tourism values and the increased community conflict related to current tourism practices result from numerous "disruptions" to this idealized American vision. And yet these disruptions to our more monolithic view of our heritage have themselves been largely contained and "historicized" by heritage professionals as they account for societal changes — so that, in a very real sense, we have traded the elite nationalism of the later 19th century for a new and highly relativistic and secularized view of heritage. This newly evolved view, however, while more resonant to the liberal values that many of us (myself included) hold dear, is nonetheless often just as partial in its realization and as potentially dominating in its practice.

Some Prospects of Heritage

I find that I am now old enough to have acquired some sense of heritage in my own right. It has been my privilege to have spent a good part of my life in close association with two major pieces of water — the northwestern United States' Puget Sound of my youth and the Chesapeake Bay environs of my present. Both coasts have seen dramatic transformations in the past half century. When I first came to live in Edmonds, Washington, in the early 1950s, the chief public value of Puget Sound was its picture-window view from a distance. The beach areas themselves were devoted largely to commercial and industrial activities, were in parts fairly derelict, and were little frequented for recreational purposes other than fishing. Today, the town's waterfront is completely different, devoted largely to upscale tourism and built around a heritage aesthetic that celebrates cosmopolitan and maritime themes that have scant relationship to anything that I can recall from my youth — a childhood that started in association with the marginal farming and make-do occupations of so many of my own relatives. The place even smells different, and I can find very little of my own inheritances in its present. What my home town has become is not all that bad, understand; it is just not what it purports to be — it has created a past and a sense of heritage distinction that has less and less to do with anything it ever was. The other past, the things I do remember, have much less of a public presence, and are captured mostly in chance encounters with old friends, occasional family reunions, and faded photographs.

I have, of course, opted for another way in life and, along with many others of these times, I have chosen to separate myself from my place and at least partly from my inheritance. In this respect I represent the extra modernity that I am now writing about — one more of the drifting, center-less, relativistic, and perhaps homeless souls, so typical of those professionals to whom we have wittingly or not entrusted the constructions of our heritages and, through those constructions, also perhaps surrendered too much of our future.

I do not think the Chesapeake Bay is much different from the locales of my youth. Even in the twenty years and then some that I have been here, I have seen dramatic changes to the look and feel of many places on the Bay, and those are just the superficial parts of it. Deeper still run the fading memories of what it all once smelled like, felt like, really looked like, and what it conveyed into the hearts of its communities — subtle but profound relocations of place and consciousness that in the long run are bound to be as important a part of the Bay's destiny as were the effects of those long ago glacial retreats that first formed the Bay.

The idea that heritage and inheritance are not just about the past but are also wholly connected to our present and to our future is important here. By representing heritage predominantly in terms of history, it is easy to forget or neglect these connections and to create senses of heritage that bear little resemblance to either the pasts or presents of their localities. I prefer to think of heritage in cultural terms because the very idea of cultural process encourages us to consider particular associations with the past as they are actually realized in the present and employed as guidelines to the future — that is, associations actively realized and used by the specific heirs of particular places, occupations, and life ways. Culture, not history, is the glue of human memory, connecting place and value to people's recollections in ways that make the past not only meaningful but also practically useful to its specific heirs.

With modernization we have seen the emergence of a more "public" sense of heritage-as-history that is not necessarily well connected to the daily lives of localized communities. These representations of heritage are often created to serve specific state interests, whether those be the drive for national cohesion that was apparent during early modern times, or the more contemporary preoccupation with interests related to promoting such values as diversity, multiculturism, and environmental moderation, or simply to fulfill the state's interest in sustained economic growth. As I claimed in respect to changes in my hometown of Edmonds, these general uses of heritage are not in and of themselves necessarily bad or injurious things, and they can have quite beneficial results in terms of economic development, public education, and encouraging people to care more responsibly for the experiences of others and for their environment. The danger, however, is that we come to think of this more public and thoroughly mediated sense of heritage as being adequately representative of the heritages and inheritances of real people — the sights, smells, places, etiquettes, and conduct that actually help people and communities move their lives from one day to the next.

So we have, as I suggested at the beginning of this essay, two senses of heritage. The one — more public, based in history and usually beyond our effective control — serves primarily to introduce us to things that are outside our immediate experience. It might well be that such ways of connecting to and interpreting the past are necessary conditions of a world that has become as complex and multidimensional as ours. This kind of heritage is a story told to us by others, usually some kind of professional intermediary, for quite specific purposes, such as to convince us to behave in a certain way, respect something that is beyond our evident self-interest, or perhaps purchase some product or experience. This is the kind of heritage representation that I have described through much of this essay.

Then there is the other sense of heritage and inheritance that I have alluded to, which greatly precedes the other, is more private and more cultural than historical, and which cannot exist as a birthright independent of the ability of its specific heirs to control it. This is the kind of heritage that can be jeopardized when local images, ceremonies, and properties are moved from their status as direct inheritances into the more public sphere of heritage production. Heritage in this sense is that part of a community's past, realized in practices and values, that the community itself recognizes as being necessary to its continuance and well-being. When others capture the means by which such an inheritance normally occurs, this can contribute to the dissolution of community and the alienation of heritage. Individuals and communities struggle against this takeover and adopt whatever means might be available to try to maintain their inheritances, often furtively through activities that are of little interest to outsiders, such as family reunions and gatherings, church meetings, and letters from home, but sometimes also through dissent and protest.[49]

A brief example might help demonstrate the precarious relationship between these two senses of heritage. Let us consider once more some of the Chesapeake Bay's watermen and women communities, besieged on the one hand by threats to their livelihood due to the depletion of various fisheries, and in some cases by the actual physical erosion of their places, and yet celebrated widely as a symbol of the Bay's distinct and colorful maritime history. If we try to look at this situation from the perspective of the watermen, we can envision at least two choices. The one option is for watermen communities to buy into the very public "folklorization" of their inheritances, learning in the process to view their own culture in fairly static terms, the core of which is dependent upon a limited range of practices and occupational specializations that are becoming less feasible. This choice is one of learning to accept one's own demise. But another option for the watermen is to recognize the limitations of the popular, heavily historied images of them, and to acknowledge the extent to which they have survived as people, families, and communities, not through any specific (now memorialized) practices but through the expression of a culture of resilience and adaptability — survival strategies that have provided them with a very different kind of distinction and that can continue to serve them well into the future.

Fifty years ago, a major issue concerning heritage was how it served to define any of us. During the late 1950s, the Argentine author Jorge Luis Borges confronted his critics, who had accused Borges of denying his patrimony and failing to be an *Argentine* writer because he chose to write on universal rather than parochial themes. He wrote:

> [W]e should essay all themes, and we cannot limit ourselves to purely Argentine subjects in order to be Argentine; for either being Argentine is an inescapable act of fate — and in that case we shall be so in all events — or being Argentine is mere affectation, a mask.[50]

Half a century later, the Japanese American architect Arata Isozaki came to a different conclusion in trying to locate his particular artistry:

> I can't be Japanese and I can't be Western — but I understand both. I am double-binded, but — and this is perhaps most important — I am also in a position that generates a great deal of energy and creativity.[51]

For Borges, heritage seems inalienable. It is either there or it is not, and celebrating it does not seem to make much difference either way. For Isozaki, on the other hand, heritage has become an instrument, leading in his case to a kind of creative energy. It is useful not because it defines him in a particular way, but because it enables him to imagine new definitions for things, and perhaps also for himself. For both Borges and Isozaki, heritage is a private thing, elusive yet also sure, and really no one else's business.

I have suggested in several parts of this essay that a more natural sense of heritage and inheritance conveys not only certain rights and privileges, but also a range of obligations to both the past and the present — so that as an inheritor and a descendent, a person or a community becomes the living rep-

resentation of a particular life way. Modern, more public heritage representations threaten to weaken these links, at least to the extent that communities
and persons might come to believe that they no longer have control over their
own heritages and inheritances. To the extent that such an alienation can,
through the protocols of inheritance discussed in the early parts of this essay,
result in a sense of a loss of birthright, so might communities and individuals
experience heightened threats to their relative autonomy. They may face an
erosion of their right to occupy particular places, to have access to the human
and natural resources that have customarily sustained them, and to relate to
the rest of the world in a manner that is respectful of those interdependencies
with others who have contributed their resilience and survivability.

Another issue that is worth a moment's reflection has to do with the discussion within this essay of the important role played by a variety of professionals in contributing to the discovery, authentication, measures of significance, and public representations associated with heritage. I have argued here
that the role of heritage professionals has been largely to "historicize" and
"public-ize" elements of heritage, many of which were once held as private
inheritances. While the late modern goals of using heritage have included
attention to diversity and to advocating for community-based participatory
processes in heritage matters, it seems that most of the professions and occupations associated with heritage and its exploitation have changed very little,
continuing to negotiate heritage properties in the interests of the state and its
elite sponsors, along with the presumed interests of a vaguely realized and
largely inert public. Still, I do not advocate an abolition of these professions or
their practices, which seem a necessary part of the complex world in which we
find ourselves. We are, perhaps, dependent upon others to inform us as to how
we might yet be related to those other heritages through which we pass, to help
us gain perspective and to help instill in us some measure of toleration and
respect for those questions of fundamental meaning that occur when our values collide with the values of others. I believe that heritage professionals are in
general getting better at this mission, becoming more reflexive in their consul-
tations, and more critically aware of their own role in the production of heritage *things* as well as heritage *values*.

But what of this other, more private sense of heritage and inheritance that
seems so vulnerable to the public heritages we have created? Is there anything
more that heritage professionals, and all of us for that matter, might do to help
protect or even restore to some of our communities those vital links of inher-

itance that seem so necessary to the maintenance of local communities, providing access to a heritage and a future over which people have some significant measure of local control? The first step is to recognize that such a sense of heritage does exist and that it is different from the kinds of heritage production in which we have become so deeply invested. This more private heritage is less a part of public history and more a cultural process that has routinely and for a very long time provided local distinction and protected birthright. From this point, there are additional practices that can be encouraged:

- *A better understanding of culturally based heritage and inheritance.* Through the disciplined practice of ethnography, a method of inquiry that has developed in relation to the study of culture and cultural processes, we can better understand culturally based heritage and the actual ways in which communities select from their pasts in order to inform their present and future.

  To date, much of the "discovery" of heritage has been invested in the special interests of heritage professionals, to the extent that the kind of heritage revealed has depended on what kind of heritage professional has been engaged in its discovery. Different heritages and markers of heritage will be provided, for example, by folklorists, archaeologists, cultural anthropologists, fine arts coordinators, tourism planners, environmentalists, or historic preservationists. Ethnography, although never free of its own biases, does provide a means for teasing out those connections of the past to the present that are actually meaningful to and sustained through the practices of community members. These heritage and inheritance connections are likely to be different from the particular focus emphasized by heritage professionals.[52]

- *Participation of Heritage Communities.* Critical attention needs to be paid to ways in which heritage professions have attempted to engage the participation of heritage communities. Recognition of the needs for "public participation" and for encouraging community-based initiative in the identification and exploitation of heritage resources represents a start in this direction. Unfortunately, we have little understanding of what actually happens when such goals are engaged, or of how to account for variability in community responses. Many if not most recent participatory initiatives have proven disappointing. The development of effective participatory processes will require systematic evaluation of such efforts and the adoption of a more critical focus on how certain heritage professionals actually relate to communities where they are involved. Equally important is the need to better understand how the values and practices of heritage professions are shaped by conditions of employment and sponsorship.

• *A better understanding of the relationships between public heritage and private inheritances.* There are several dimensions to such an understanding. We need, for example, to better recognize the extent to which heritage professionals conduct their labors in respect to acquired disciplinary preferences, and to realize that they are stakeholders in their own right rather than neutral or objective bystanders. We also need to better appreciate the differences between most contemporary promotions of public heritage with their more relativistic views and the necessarily value-laden, durable, and often "intolerant" perspectives associated with the inheritances of localized communities. We should look for and try to understand those cases in which these perspectives might come into conflict, as well as seek better means to resolve competition and frictions between public representation of heritage and the direct inheritance value of the past.

• *A better sense of the ways in which the local community will present its face in the future.* An improved understanding of local communities will foster the kinds of associations that help maintain our cultural inheritances. After all, localized communities are not really the antithesis to the forces of modernization, and the partisan and exclusive values that they represent are a necessary part of the modern. Even the most seemingly traditional communities are never static, and there really is no such thing as being culturally deprived or "backward" or "losing" one's culture. The ability to form localized communities of the kind described in this essay seems essential to maintaining our capacity for establishing meaningful, rewarding, and reasonable associations of any kind. The recognition of the interdependence of such local communities is of equal importance. The effects of modernization alone, which include such phenomena as the celebration of public heritage, will always seem superficial and only partially realized in comparison to the more deeply experienced practices of localized, culturally informed communities.

• *A realization that heritage is ultimately a human creation.* It will serve us well to recognize without prejudice that localized heritage and inheritance are finally particular kinds of cultural fiction and therefore inescapably "false," partisan, and biased, and that this is not a weakness but a strength. The standards used for judging the authenticity and significance of public heritage cannot apply to establishing the "truths" of more localized inheritances, which derive their usefulness from their narratives and are based upon an exercise of faith rather than of evidence.[53] As David Lowenthal has suggested:

> Heritage is not a testable or even plausible version of our past; it is a declaration of faith in the past.... Prejudiced pride in the past is not the sorry upshot of heritage but its essential aim.... Heritage diverges from history not in being biased but in its view of bias. Historians aim to reduce bias; heritage sanctions and strengthens it.[54]

Culturally based inheritance, unlike most public heritage, derives its power from the control its heirs exhibit over the telling of its contemporary meanings, a control which is not subject to the same standards of proof or credibility as might be applied to public heritage, and which is continually exercised in such a way as to fill reason with good sense and the fulfillment of purpose.

The final point to be offered is simply to advocate once again for the recognition of two quite different ideas about heritage, both of value to us for different reasons, and to caution against the tendency to let one sense of heritage, more public and easily viewed, subsume the interests and power of the other. Such a domination can, of course, occur only in our minds, because in actuality our more private inheritances cannot be so easily disregarded. The danger is that a failure to recognize the importance and value of localized heritage and inheritance processes can contribute to other forms of political and economic domination that do have the power to do harm to communities — including those of the Chesapeake Bay country — and to alter the circumstances of all our lives.

Notes

1. This does not imply that social and environmental processes, though clearly linked, operate in an ecosystem in the same way or according to similar regularities or laws, although such parallels are often assumed in the environmental literature. This issue will be discussed later in this essay.

2. It would require another essay to spell out the practical implications of these two different views. For example, they can shape the ways in which social and economic policies are devoted to assisting communities at risk, varying from policies that assume that people lack local resources and need to learn new skills, to other policies that aim to identify and build upon a community's existing "assets." As I will suggest toward the end of this essay, the ways in which heritage is reconstructed can have important effects on the thinking of the people to whom particular heritages are attributed.

3. The numerous historic churches and revival sites of the Chesapeake Bay region have the potential to serve as markers of some of the earliest traditions of Christian worship in the United States. We might well ask why they have not been more generally exploited for tourism or slated for greater public recognition. One guess would be that the increased secularization and state sponsorship of heritage identification and reconstruction contributes to an ambivalence in regard to featuring sacred sites. The same might well apply to the ways in which Chesapeake Bay folklore is often depicted without reference to the strong religious sentiments that inform the lives of the residents of many Chesapeake Bay communities. There are exceptions, as in the example just provided in the body of this essay, as well as in the occasional folkloric presentation of Bay area gospel traditions and the touristic promotion of local religious festivals.

4. David Lowenthal. The Past is a Foreign Country (Cambridge, England: Cambridge University Press, 1985).

5. Eric Hobsbawm and Terence Ranger, eds., The Invention of Tradition (Cambridge, England: Cambridge University Press, 1984).

6. Benedict Anderson, Imagined Communities: Reflections on the Origin and Spread of Nationalism (London: Verso, 1991).

7. Even the titles of these authors' best known works are evocative of the transient and constructed nature of heritage: The Past is a Foreign Country (Lowenthal),

The Invention of Tradition (Hobsbawn and Ranger), and Imagined Communities (Anderson).

8. By "early modernity" and "early modern" I refer to the period of rapid industrialization and economic transformation that came to dominate much of the world during the last half of the 19th century and through World War I. My usage is not to be confused with archaeology's designation of the Early Modern (AD 1750-1850) period of New World Archaeology.

9. Adele V. Holden, Down on the Shore: The Family and Place that Forged a Poet's Voice (Centreville, Maryland: Tidewater Publishers, 2003).

10. I will use the term "localized community" in contrast to modern urbanized/globalized communities and in place of such choices as "traditional" or "premodern" communities. While localized communities predominated prior to modern times, they still exist and even thrive within modern settings. In fact, one of the major sources of conflict in the negotiation of contemporary issues pertaining to heritage lies in the struggle between forces of localization and those of modernity and globalization.

11. In my usage, the term "local" is not at all the same as "place" or dependent upon some specific geographic residence. One way to think of the local would be as a community of interest, or simply as a group of people who feel that they maintain enough common value and similarity of prospect to constitute themselves as a meaningful (i.e., cultural) group. A localized community could consist of some of the members of an actual neighborhood, or it could as well be formed of interest groups who communicate solely on the Internet and never meet face to face, or others who identify with each other in respect to ethnic or other realms of experience.

12. David Boswell and Jessica Evans, Representing the Nation: A Reader (New York: Routledge, 1999).

13. Thomas F. King, Patricia Parker Hickman, and Gary Berg, Anthropology in Historic Preservation: Caring for Culture's Clutter (New York: Academic Press, 1977); Charles B. Hosmer, Jr., Preservation of the Past: A History of the Preservation Movement in the United States Before Williamsburg (New York: G.P. Putnam's Sons, 1965).

14. Regina Bendix, In Search of Authenticity: The Formation of Folklore Studies (Madison, Wisconsin: University of Wisconsin Press, 1997).

15. Erve Chambers, Native Tours: The Anthropology of Travel and Tourism (Prospect Heights, Illinois: Waveland Press, 2000).

16. The idea of heritage as being disciplined is important here. Cultural inheritance (or the inheritance of cultural things) implies certain rights of transfer and

45

inalienability that are enjoyed by the heirs, but it also entails obligations such as the responsibility to maintain family or community ties, or the duty to protect and preserve an inheritance for future generations. These original responsibilities clearly fade when the rights of inheritance are generalized into some kind of public history. As this occurs, the state and its representatives assume much of the responsibility for the heritages they encourage. It might be said for many citizens that, while heritage is now all around them, it is in its popular manifestations increasingly less personal and something that might well interest them but for which they feel little sense of communal duty or responsibility.

17. Parker B. Potter, Jr., Public Archaeology in Annapolis: A Critical Approach to History in Maryland's Ancient City (Washington, D.C.: Smithsonian Institution Press, 1994).

18. Mark P. Leone, The Archaeology of Ideology: Archaeological Work in Annapolis Since 1981. In Paul A. Shackel and Barbara J. Little, eds., Historic Archaeology of the Chesapeake (Washington, D.C.: Smithsonian Institution Press, 1994).

19. Paul A. Shackel, Personal Discipline and Material Culture: An Archaeology of Annapolis, Maryland, 1695-1870 (Knoxville, Tennessee: University of Tennessee Press, 1993).

20. George C. Logan and Mark P. Leone, Tourism with Race in Mind: Annapolis, Maryland Examines its African American Past through Collaborative Research. In Erve Chambers, ed., Tourism and Culture: An Applied Perspective (Albany, New York: State University of New York Press, 1997).

21. Barbara J. Little, "She Was...an Example to Her Sex": Possibilities for a Feminist Historical Archaeology. In Paul A, Shackel and Barbara J. Little, eds., Historical Archaeology of the Chesapeake (Washington, D.C.: Smithsonian Institution Press, 1994).

22. Erve Chambers, Epilogue: Archaeology, Heritage, and Public Endeavor. In Paul A. Shackel and Erve Chambers, eds., Places in Mind: Public Archaeology as Applied Anthropology (New York: Routledge, 2004).

23. Richard Handler and Eric Gable, The New History in an Old Museum: Creating the Past at Colonial Williamsburg (Durham, North Carolina: Duke University Press, 1997).

24. Barbara Kirshenblatt-Gimlett, Destination Culture: Tourism, Museums, and Heritage (Berkeley, California: University of California Press, 1998).

25. In this light, it is worth considering the extent to which the increased use of sophisticated information technology in heritage settings has not only helped shape the ways in which heritage is being re-presented, but has also served to

increase the amount of control heritage professionals have over the production of heritage events and displays.

26. Eric Gable, Richard Handler, and Anna Lawson, On the Uses of Relativism: Fact, Conjecture, and Black and White at Colonial Williamsburg, American Ethnologist 19(4): 791-805, 1992.

27. Kathy Borland, Hispanic Cultural-Religious Traditions. In T. Walker, ed., Folk Arts & Cultural Traditions of the Delmarva Peninsula: An Interpretive Resource Guide (Baltimore, Maryland: Mid Atlantic Arts Foundation, 2003).

28. Heritage can take strange twists indeed. Terry Plowman (1999) has noted that many recent Latino immigrants to the Delmarva peninsula have brought with them evangelical religious practices that have a surprising similarity to many of the peninsula's earliest religious traditions.

29. David Griffith, The Estuary's Gift: An Atlantic Coast Cultural Biography (University Park, Pennsylvania: The Pennsylvania State University Press, 1999).

30. John Urry, Consuming Places (London: Routledge, 1995).

31. Arnold R. Alanen and Robert Z. Melnick, Preserving Cultural Landscapes in America (Baltimore, Maryland: Johns Hopkins University Press, 2000).

32. We will have occasion to discuss the transition from criteria of authenticity to those of significance at the end of this section. Shifts in the ways in which heritage is given location or direction, as in the recent popularity of heritage areas and corridors, trails, and waterways, provide a great opportunity to see heritage in the process of its construction. For example, the Eastern Shore's Beach to Bay Indian Trail was placed in service more than a decade ago and has only begun to assume any kind of heritage identity in its own right.

33. Arif Dirlik, Place-Based Imagination: Globalism and the Politics of Place. In R. Praznink and A. Dirlik, eds., Places and Politics in an Age of Globalization (New York: Rowman & Littlefield Publishers, 2001).

34. Arjun Appadurai, Modernity at Large: Cultural Dimensions of Globalization (Minneapolis, Minnesota: University of Minnesota Press, 1996).

35. Paul Hawken, Armony Lovins, and L. Hunter Lovins, Natural Capitalism: Creating the Next Industrial Revolution (Boston, Massachusetts: Little, Brown and Company, 1999); Theodore Roszak, The Voice of the Earth: An Exploration of Ecopsychology (York Beach, Maine: Phanes Press, 2002).

36. This shift from an equilibrium model to one that recognizes "natural" imbalances in ecological systems has parallels to other conceptual turns described in earlier parts of the essay, such as the new social history and the idea of culture as a

dynamic and essentially unstable process. Such a concurrence testifies to the degree to which our conceptualizations of natural and human social processes are reflected overall in cultural shifts in the paradigms that we use to explain our world to ourselves. There is some desirable neatness to such epistemologically interesting parallels, but there are also dangers. There is, for example, no clear evidence that "natural" and "cultural" processes work in similar fashion, although they certainly influence each other in important ways. I provide one example of a possible discrepancy later in this section when I discuss the concepts of ecological and human diversity. Another example is at least implied in my earlier discussion of changes in the ways we have come to conceptualize culture, moving away from an analogy with biological evolutionary processes to recognize that humans create meaningful cultural distinctions in quite different ways from those envisioned in nature.

37. Kenneth R. Olwig, The Nature of Cultural Heritage and the Culture of Natural Heritage (New York: Routledge, 2006).

38. Ted Bernard and Jora Young, The Ecology of Hope: Communities Collaborate for Sustainability (Gabriola Island, British Columbia: New Society Publishers, 1997).

39. Donald Worster, Nature and the Disorder of History. In M.E. Soule and Gary Lease, eds., Reinventing Nature? Responses to Postmodern Deconstruction (Washington, D.C.: Island Press, 1995).

40. David Griffith. The Estuary's Gift.

41. Michael Paolisso, Blue Crabs and Controversy on the Chesapeake Bay: A Cultural Model for Understanding Watermen's Reasoning about Blue Crab Management, Human Organization 61(3):226-239 (2002).

42. This would suggest that any attempt to co-manage a natural resource, such as the Chesapeake Bay blue crab, would require more than a solicitation of the opinions of various stakeholders. To be effective, such a plan would require an appreciation of stakeholder heritage and the positing of an ethic that respected both the "public good" and the expectations rooted in local inheritances.

43. The issues related to the repatriation of remains and artifacts from the nation's museums to Native Americans serve as a vivid example of the problems associated with both identifying the heirs and the property rights of pieces of heritage.

44. While this shift accurately reflects a tendency toward less intimacy with the locations of tourism on the part of most tourists, it does not discount the more adventuresome tourist who deliberately seeks closer associations with local people and place.

45. John R. Wennersten, Maryland's Eastern Shore: A Journey in Time and Place (Centreville, Maryland: Tidewater Publishers, 1992).

46. Alison K. Hoagland, Industrial Housing and Vinyl Siding: Historical Significance Flexibly Applied. In M.A. Tomlan, ed., Preservation for What, for Whom? (Ithaca, New York: The National Council for Preservation Education, 1999).

47. C. John Sullivan, Water Fowling on the Chesapeake: 1819-1936 (Baltimore: Maryland: Johns Hopkins University Press, 2003).

48. Attempts to preserve and benefit from earlier tourism traditions around the Chesapeake have occurred in respect to Baltimore's Bay Shore Park (now North Point State Park) and in the upper Eastern Shore communities of Betterton and Tolchester. Tolchester Beach's amusement park was opened in 1877, serving primarily the populace of Baltimore, and closed in 1962. It is now the site of a museum memorializing the resort.

49. Since the more private natural inheritances that I have discussed here are so readily subsumed by more public heritages, we often fail to recognize the forms of resistance and protests that can accompany a sense of their loss. Although it does not apply to the Bay, Jeremy Boissevan's (1996) account of the ways in which European communities react to the appropriation of their heritages through tourism initiatives is insightful.

50. Jorge Luis Borges, Labyrinths: Selected Stories & Other Writings (New York: New Directions Publishing Corporation, 1962).

51. Isozaki is quoted in Pico Iyer, The Global Soul (New York: Alfred A. Knopf, 2000).

52. Variation between professionally developed heritage and community-based heritage can be related to actual practices as well as to values through which heritage is viewed by a community. The family reunion is an example of a heritage practice that has received little recognition or support from the heritage professions. The presence of the sacred and the centrality of political ideologies are examples of how localized heritage and inheritance can be framed in a values perspective that is often missed or set aside by outsiders. For example, the practice of the Chesapeake Bay waterman's occupation is partially realized through the traditional tools and historical experiences related to their fishery — common subjects of public heritage — but is also made manifest in the perspectives of many watermen, perspectives made meaningful and consequential only through the lens of a religious belief system and a foundation of conservative values that have been largely ignored by their more liberal and secular-minded professional mediators.

53. The exercise of faith suggested here might be expressed through formal religious beliefs or by more existential means, as suggested by Soren Kirkegaard's "leap of faith," or even simply by the practices of trust and reliance that inform many community relations.

54. David Lowenthal, Fabricating Heritage, History and Memory, Volume 10, Number 1, pp 1-16 (2003).

References

Anderson, Benedict. 1991. Imagined Communities: Reflections on the Origin and Spread of Nationalism. London: Verso.

Appadurai, Arjun. 1996. Modernity at Large: Cultural Dimensions of Globalization. Minneapolis, Minnesota: University of Minnesota Press.

Bendix, Regina. 1997. In Search of Authenticity: The Formation of Folklore Studies. Madison, Wisconsin: University of Wisconsin Press.

Bernard, Ted and Jora Young. 1997. The Ecology of Hope: Communities Collaborate for Sustainability. Gabriola Island, British Columbia: New Society Publishers.

Boissevain, Jeremy, Ed. 1996. Coping with Tourists: European Reactions to Mass Tourism. Providence, Rhode Island: Berghahan Books.

Boswell, David and Jessica Evans. 1999. Representing the Nation: A Reader. New York: Routledge.

Chambers, Erve. 2004. Epilogue: Archaeology, Heritage, and Public Endeavor. In Paul A. Shackel and Erve Chambers, eds., Places in Mind: Public Archaeology as Applied Anthropology. New York: Routledge.

Chambers, Erve. 2000. Native Tours: The Anthropology of Travel and Tourism. Prospect Heights, Illinois: Waveland Press.

Gable, Eric, Richard Handler, and Anna Lawson. 1992. On the Uses of Relativism: Fact, Conjecture, and Black and White at Colonial Williamsburg. American Ethnologist 19(4): 791-805.

Griffith, David. 1999. The Estuary's Gift: An Atlantic Coast Cultural Biography. University Park, Pennsylvania: The Pennsylvania State University Press.

Handler, Richard and Eric Gable. 1997. The New History in an Old Museum: Creating the Past at Colonial Williamsburg. Durham, North Carolina: Duke University Press.

Hawken, Paul, Armony Lovins, and L. Hunter Lovins. 1999. Natural Capitalism: Creating the Next Industrial Revolution. Boston, Massachusetts: Little, Brown and Company.

Hoagland, Alison K. 1999. Industrial Housing and Vinyl Siding: Historical Significance Flexibly Applied. In M.A. Tomlan, ed., Preservation For What, For Whom? Ithaca, New York: The National Council for Preservation Education.

Hobsbawm, Eric and Terence Ranger, eds. 1984. The Invention of Tradition. Cambridge, England: Cambridge University Press.

Horton, Tom. 1987. Bay Country. Baltimore, Maryland: Johns Hopkins University Press.

Hosmer, Charles B., Jr. 1965. Preservation of the Past: A History of the Preservation Movement in the United States Before Williamsburg. G.P. Putnam's Sons: New York.

King, Thomas F., Patricia Parker Hickman and Gary Berg. 1977. Anthropology in Historic Preservation: Caring for Culture's Clutter. New York: Academic Press.

Kirshenblatt-Gimblett, Barbara. 1998. Destination Culture: Tourism, Museums, and Heritage. Berkeley, California: University of California Press.

Leone, Mark P. 1994. The Archaeology of Ideology: Archaeological Work in Annapolis since 1981. In Paul A. Shackel and Barbara J. Little, eds., Historic Archaeology of the Chesapeake. Washington, D.C: Smithsonian Institution Press.

Little, Barbara J. 1994. "She Was...an Example to Her Sex": Possibilities for a Feminist Historical Historical Archaeology. In Paul A, Shackel and Barbara J. Little, eds., Historical Archaeology of the Chesapeake. Washington, D.C: Smithsonian Institution Press.

Logan, George C. and Mark P. Leone. 1997. Tourism with Race in Mind: Annapolis, Maryland Examines its African American Past through Collaborative Research. In Erve Chambers, ed., Tourism and Culture: An Applied Perspective. Albany, New York: State University of New York Press.

Lowenthal, David. 1985. The Past is a Foreign Country. Cambridge, England: Cambridge University Press.

Lowenthal, David. 2003. Fabricating Heritage, History and Memory, Volume 10, Number 1, pp 1-16.

Paolisso, Michael. 2002. Blue Crabs and Controversy on the Chesapeake Bay: A Cultural Model for Understanding Watermen's Reasoning about Blue Crab Management. Human Organization 61(3):226-239.

Plowman, Terry. 1999. Delmarva's Religious History. In Terry Plowman, ed., Delmarva Milllennium, Vol. 1. Salisbury, Maryland: Thomson-Chesapeake.

Prazniak, Roxann and Arif Dirlik, eds. 2001. Places and Politics in an Age of Globalization. Lanham, Maryland: Rowland & Littlefield Publishers.

Potter, Parker B., Jr. 1994. Public Archaeology in Annapolis: A Critical Approach to History in Maryland's Ancient City. Washington, D.C: Smithsonian Institution Press.

Roszak, Theodore. 2002. The Voice of the Earth: An Exploration of Ecopsychology. York Beach, Maine: Phanes Press.

Shackel, Paul A. 1993. Personal Discipline and Material Culture: An Archaeology of Annapolis, Maryland, 1695-1870. Knoxville, Tennessee: University of Tennessee Press.

Sullivan, C. John. 2003. Water Fowling on the Chesapeake: 1819-1936. Baltimore, Maryland: Johns Hopkins University Press.

Turner, William H. 1998. East of the Chesapeake. Baltimore, Maryland: Johns Hopkins University Press.

Urry, John. 1995. Consuming Places. London: Routledge.

Walker, Tom. 2003. Folk Arts and Cultural Traditions of the Delmarva Peninsula: An Interpretive Resource Guide. Baltimore, Maryland: Mid Atlantic Arts Foundation.

Warner, William H. 1976. Beautiful Swimmers: Watermen, Crabs and the Chesapeake Bay. Boston, Massachusetts: Little, Brown and Company.

Wennersten, John R. 1992. Maryland's Eastern Shore: A Journey in Time and Place. Centreville, Maryland: Tidewater Publishers.

Acknowledgments

I want to thank Jonathan Kramer and Jack Greer of Maryland Sea Grant for their support and encouragement, as well as their patience in helping realize this monograph. Michael Paolisso is my colleague and good guide to thinking about the Chesapeake and I do appreciate his insights and advice. Helpful suggestions in response to an early draft of this monograph were made by colleagues Judith Freidenberg, Shawn Maloney, Amanda Mason, Yixin Qiu, Rosemary Riel, and Paul Shackel.

About This Monograph Series

This monograph is part of a series entitled *Chesapeake Perspectives*, produced by the University of Maryland Sea Grant College to encourage researchers, scholars, and other thinkers to share their insights into the unique culture and ecology of the Chesapeake Bay. Its audience includes environmental scientists and scholars, from marine biologists to cultural anthropologists, and a broad interested public that encompasses resource managers, watershed organizations, and citizen advocates. For more about future books in the series and related topics, visit the web at www.mdsg.umd.edu.